MW01096677

Science Tutor: Life Science

By

GARY RAHAM

COPYRIGHT © 2005 Mark Twain Media, Inc.

ISBN-13: 978-1-58037-307-4
ISBN-10: 1-58037-307-0

Printing No. CD-404034

Mark Twain Media, Inc., Publishers
Distributed by Carson-Dellosa Publishing Company, Inc.

Table of Contents

Introduction/How to Use This Book

Enjoy exploring life science topics under four broad categories included in modern science teaching standards: (1) Patterns in the Living World; (2) Energy Flow in Living Systems; (3) The Human Animal and Levels of Organization; and (4) Descent and Change.

Section 1 deals with organizing and classifying living things, an overview of life's diversity, and the patterns and cycles of ecosystems. *Section 2* follows the energy flow and chemistries of living systems. *Section 3* focuses on human placement in the biosphere, human functioning at the organ and organ system levels, and the role of diseases. *Section 4* discusses patterns of development and reproduction, heredity, and the role of extinctions in life's changing cast of characters over time.

Key terms appear **boldfaced** in the text. *Absorb* sections introduce new concepts. *Apply* sections allow the reader to exercise his or her knowledge of the content and concepts by answering questions, filling in the blanks, and engaging in short activities. At the end of each section, the reader is invited to "put it all together" and test his or her understanding of that section.

Because a lot of ground is covered in a short space, the visuals become especially important. Good illustrations and diagrams certainly do convey a large portion of the informational content and serve to organize ideas in a readily absorbable form.

Name: _____ Date: _____

Part 1: Patterns in the Living World: Making Sense of Life's Diversity

We live within a thin film of living things on a rocky planet called Earth. This thin film of life is called the **biosphere**. Microscopic creatures mark the boundaries of this sphere. Things like bacteria, spores, and even baby spiders float in the air miles above us. Primitive cells deep within rock use chemicals to fuel their lives. We live right in the middle of the action, interacting with Rover and other pets, eating an assortment of plants and animals, and serving as hosts for some critters that like to live in or on us. Millions of other unseen creatures recycle chemicals necessary to keep the entire biosphere alive. How can a person make sense of this huge assortment of living things?

We could organize or **classify** life in many ways: by color, by size, by whether we can eat it (or it wants to eat us), or whether it makes us sick. Our distant ancestors probably used many of these systems to organize other creatures in ways that would keep themselves and their families alive and healthy. Any good classification system should be *meaningful* to those using it, *easily understood*, and *easy to describe* to someone else.

By the eighteenth century, as humans began to explore the world in detail, it became apparent that living things shared similarities in structure or **anatomy** that were probably more meaningful than superficial appearance or how they lived. In the mid-1700s, a Swedish scientist named **Carolus Linnaeus** did much of the early work classifying living things by similarities in form. A half-century later, a Frenchman, **Georges Cuvier**, showed how the form of living animals could be linked to creatures that lived long ago but died before there were humans to see them.

APPLY:

1. List ten different kinds of living things with which you interacted within the last 24 hours:

   _____ _____ _____ _____ _____

   _____ _____ _____ _____ _____

2. Devise a system that would divide the ten living things above into three or more groups that would be useful to your best friend, would make sense to him or her, and would be easy to understand. Write the system on your own paper.

3. Aristotle, a "natural philosopher" of the fourth century B.C., divided living things into animals and plants. He further divided animals into those that could walk, those that could fly, and those that could swim. Name five animals that would fit in the "animals that fly" category:

   _____ _____ _____ _____ _____

   Do any of these seem "out of place" or too dissimilar to belong together? Why or why not?

   _____

4. Name two early scientists who made important contributions to the classification of living

   things. _____ _____

Name: _____ Date: _____

Classifying and Naming Living Things

 Carolus Linnaeus hit upon the idea of giving each living thing a unique, two-part name that describes the particular kind of creature it is (its **species**) and also a group name (called a **genus**) that includes other quite similar species. Both parts of a creature's scientific name are taken mostly from Latin, a "dead" language that doesn't change over time. Scientists of all nationalities learn to recognize the same Latin names for organisms. Human beings are called *Homo sapiens*, which literally means "Man, wise." Note that the genus (in this case *Homo*) is always capitalized, but the species name is not. Both words are italicized. Modern humans have no other species in their genus, but extinct members of our species have been identified in the fossil record. This two-part naming system is called **binomial nomenclature**.

Linnaeus recognized two very large **kingdoms** of living things: animals and plants. He also recognized progressively larger groupings of creatures above the genus level called **families**, **orders**, and **classes**. A family may contain several orders, an order may contain a number of classes, and a class may have many genera (the plural of genus). Georges Cuvier, mentioned earlier, later added the category of phylum. A **phylum** may contain various families. Think of these groupings as nested containers, one within the other like the illustration to the right.

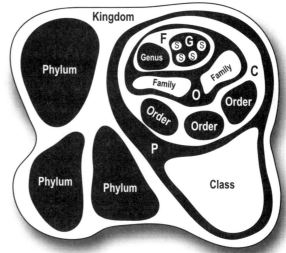

The order of kingdom, phylum, class, order, family, genus, and species can be remembered by thinking of the phrase "**K**ings **p**lay **c**ards **o**n **f**ast, **g**ray **s**hips."

APPLY:

1. *Canis familiaris* is the scientific name of the dog. Which of the following creatures is most similar to the dog? _____

   A. *Felis onca*   B. *Mus musculus*   C. *Canis latrans*   D. *Felis concolor*

   Which of the other animals in this list share a common genus? _____ and _____

2. The phylum vertebrata contains all animals with backbones. Which of the following animals would you expect to be in a different phylum?

   A. Whale   B. Bat   C. Dragonfly   D. Kangaroo

3. Which plants do you think are most similar? _____

   A. Skeleton weed and salsify, which are in the same family

   B. Magnolia and buttercups, which are in the same class

The Five Living Kingdoms

Today scientists recognize five large kingdoms of living things: **monerans**, **protists**, **fungi**, **plants**, and **animals**. You may not have heard of some of these groups because their members are microscopic. Each kingdom seems so different at first look that it seems hard to see connections between them. However, all of Earth's life shares an identical genetic code and common repertoire of chemistries that imply a common origin.

Life's 5 Kingdoms

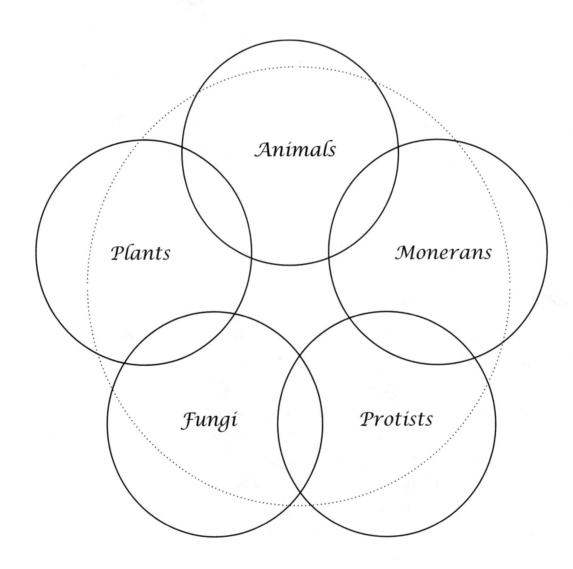

Monerans, Archaeans, and Viruses

 Most life on Earth is so small that we don't notice it until one of its representatives makes us sick. Such is the case with monerans, which include the tiny, single-celled organisms called **bacteria** and another group called the **archaea**. Moneran cells have **deoxyribonucleic acid (DNA)** and **ribonucleic acid (RNA)** as chemicals of heredity, just like our body cells, but those chemicals are not contained within the membranes of a cell nucleus. Moneran cells also lack other complex cellular machinery called **organelles**. These characteristics make monerans different from the creatures in every other kingdom.

Some bacterial cells use light energy to make sugars. Others like the archaea, use methane or other chemicals for the same purpose. Organisms that make their own food are called **autotrophs**. Organisms that must live off of other organisms (either alive or dead) are called **heterotrophs**.

Although a few species of bacteria may get out of control in human bodies and cause illness, many other kinds perform valuable functions like the *Escherichia coli* in your gut that make vitamin K. Monerans do most of the work of the world, recycling elements and producing oxygen. More bacteria live in your mouth right now than all of the humans that have ever lived. About 2.5 billion cells live in each gram of soil.

Unlike monerans, viruses cannot support themselves. They have DNA or RNA contained in a shell of protein, but they have no other cellular machinery. They must live by taking over and destroying other cells. Outside of the cells of other organisms, viruses can crystallize like a chemical. Are viruses some sort of degenerate form of moneran? Are they some kind of "almost life"? Scientists are not quite sure where they belong in a classification system for living things.

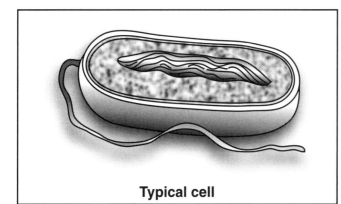

Typical cell

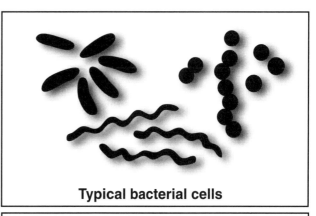

Typical bacterial cells

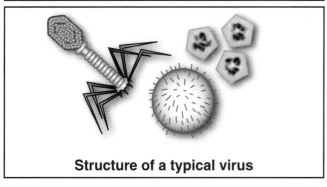

Structure of a typical virus

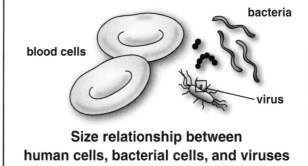

Size relationship between human cells, bacterial cells, and viruses

Protists and Fungi

Protists are single-celled creatures of great variety. Most live in fresh or saltwater habitats. Compared to a moneran cell, they are larger (think apple compared to pea) and more complex. Their DNA and RNA reside in one or more nuclei, and they have complex cell organelles made of two-layered membranes.

Heterotrophic protists come in forms that can crawl around ponds like "the blob from outer space" (**sarcodines**), dart back and forth like hairy rowboats (**ciliates**), or corkscrew through the water like a slipper with a whip-like propeller (**zooflagellates**). Autotrophs come with pigment-containing bodies like plants (**chloroplasts**). Some autotrophs look like glass pillboxes (**diatoms**), or armored diving bells (**dinoflagellates**). Others have grass-green chloroplasts in single cells, chains of cells, or globular colonies (**chlorophytes**).

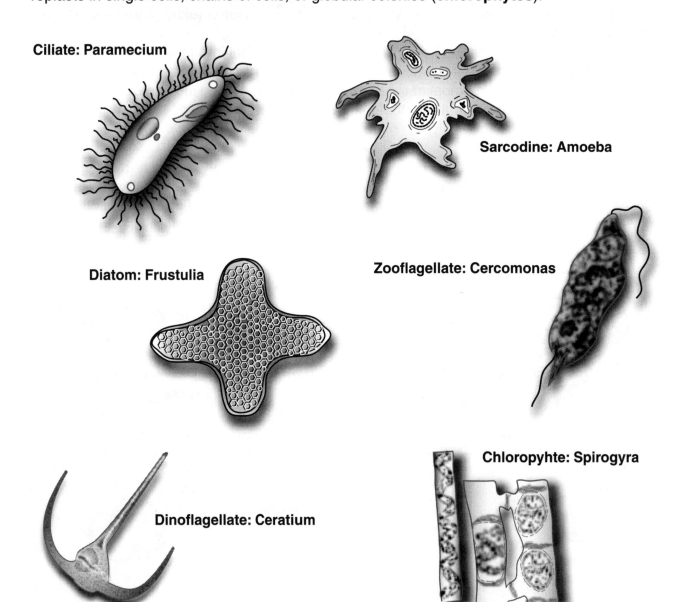

Ciliate: Paramecium

Sarcodine: Amoeba

Diatom: Frustulia

Zooflagellate: Cercomonas

Chloropyhte: Spirogyra

Dinoflagellate: Ceratium

Protists and Fungi (cont.)

You encounter the kingdom of **fungi** when a piece of bread starts supporting a growth of **molds** or when you eat a **mushroom**. If you shower a lot in a small bathroom, dark patches of **mildew** may grow on the tile or walls. Fungi are all heterotrophs that break down the dead remains of other living things. Once lumped with the plants, fungi became a distinct group when scientists learned they had some fundamental differences from green plants. Fungal cell walls are made up of different materials and hook together in long, root-like structures called **hyphae**. Hyphae also weave themselves together to form the characteristic "bodies" of the various fungi that grow on trees or pop up in your lawn after several moist days.

Fungi reproduce by shedding spores produced in sac-like structures (**ascomycetes**), club-shaped bodies (**basidiomycetes)**, or in spheres that are often at the end of long stalks (**zygomycetes**).

A large assortment of fungi have formed symbiotic associations with autotrophic cells in the moneran and protist kingdoms to form organisms called **lichens**. Lichens have a fungal body incorporating a layer of cells near the surface that often gives them a mineral green color. But they may also produce unique acids that are bright green, orange, or yellow. Lichens typically grow on, or even in, rocks and in relatively poor soils.

Typical ascomycete (mildew)

Zygomycete (black bread mold)

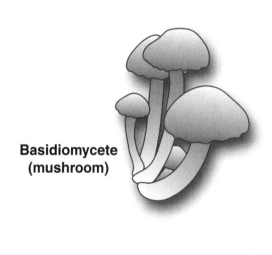

Basidiomycete (mushroom)

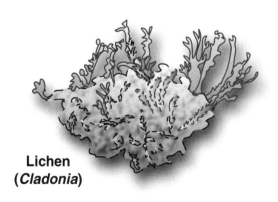

Lichen (*Cladonia*)

Animals and Plants

As animals, we all appreciate the beauty and importance of our own kingdom, forgetting that without the other kingdoms, we would quickly die. Animals are multicellular heterotrophs—dependent on other creatures for food—with cells organized into **tissues** and usually **organ systems**.

A variety of sponge-like creatures have a sac-like architecture. Food goes in a hole, nutrients get absorbed, and the waste gets shoved back out the same hole. The "wormy" body plan is a tube within a tube. Food goes in one end, nutrients are extracted, and waste goes out the other end.

One group of animals developed external skeletons like **arthropods** (includes insects, crustaceans, and spiders) and **mollusks** (includes clams, snails, squids, and the like). Vertebrate animals have bony internal skeletons. **Mammals**, like ourselves, as well as **fish**, **reptiles**, **amphibians**, and **birds** make up this group.

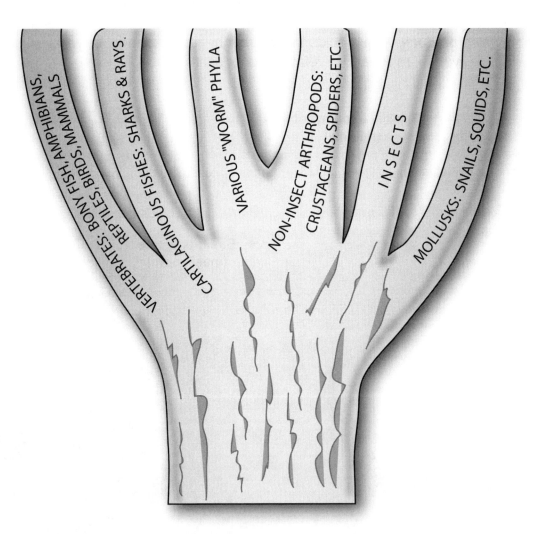

Animal Family Tree

Animals and Plants (cont.)

Plants are the large, multicellular autotrophs some animals love to eat. Plants descended from green algae in the protist kingdom. The first plants to invade dry land were small and survived without special water-carrying or **vascular** tissue. These non-vascular plants include **mosses**, **hornworts**, and **liverworts**.

Ferns are simple vascular plants whose leaves unroll like a piece of new carpet. Ferns reproduce by **spores** produced in ball-like **sporangia** found on the undersides of its compound leaves. Spores grow into small **gametophyte** plants that produce eggs and sperm that unite in a drop of water to make a new, large spore-making (**sporophyte**) generation.

Vascular plants produce **leaves**, **stems**, and **roots**. Leaves make food (**sugars**) with the help of sunlight and special pigments. Special water-transporting tissues (**xylem**) in stems provide support. **Phloem** tissues move sugars to where they are needed. Many years ago, simple, spore-bearing vascular plants related to today's tiny **horsetails** and **lycopods** had members that grew to tree size and created forests.

Gymnosperms keep eggs and sperm inside **cones**. Sperm (**pollen**) is carried to female cones with eggs (**ovules**). Egg and sperm unite to form **seeds**. Gymnosperms include plants like **conifers** and **cycads**. **Angiosperms** now rule the plant world and produce flowers. Pollen fertilizes ovules to make seeds, which are enclosed in a large, fleshy **fruit** that animals love to eat. The fruit becomes the animal's reward for spreading plant seeds around.

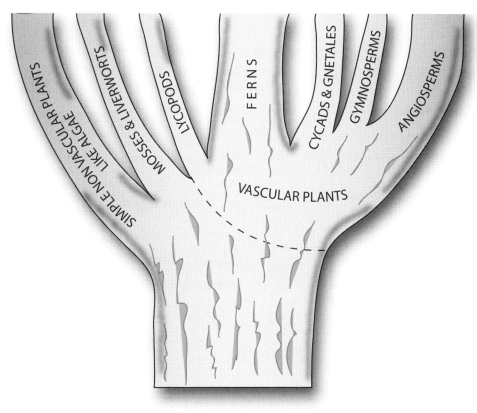

Plant Family Tree

Ecosystems

Living creatures can't survive alone. They live in a complex **community** of many organisms, large and small, along with nonliving things like water, soil, and rocks. The combination of living and nonliving elements in a given place (**habitat**) is called an **ecosystem**. Scientists may define the size of an ecosystem depending on what they wish to study. An aquatic biologist may talk about a pond ecosystem. A park ranger working in a grassland may discuss a prairie ecosystem. In truth, the entire biosphere is a complex ecosystem of **food producers**, **food consumers**, and **decomposers**.

Food producers in a prairie ecosystem consist largely of various species of grasses that exist as **populations** of individual plants of a given species. Populations of prairie dogs, voles, insects, deer, and other creatures munch on grasses, making them **first-order consumers**. **Second-order consumers** like snakes, eagles, and coyotes eat prairie dogs and voles. When producers and consumers die, decomposers convert all of the bodies to basic chemical compounds. Energy in an ecosystem flows from producers to consumers and on to decomposers.

Relationships in an ecosystem can be complex. Individuals within populations may **compete** among themselves or with other populations trying to use the same resources. Second-order consumers are often **predators** or **scavengers**. Organisms may also work together in an association called **symbiosis**, where one and/or both members of the association benefit from living together.

In the drawing of a prairie ecosystem below, draw arrows pointing from producers to consumers and from consumers to decomposers. Organisms may be connected by several arrows. When you are finished, you will have created a pattern that is called a **food web** because of its resemblance to a spider's web.

Name: _____ Date: _____

Rhythms and Cycles in the Biosphere

The earth spins, and life on its surface sees the sun arc across the sky and disappear beneath the horizon. Plants shut down food production at night, and daytime (**diurnal**) animals prepare to find shelter and sleep. Night-time (**nocturnal**) creatures emerge to take over the stage. The moon revolves around the earth in a monthly pattern that sees its face wax and wane from bright sphere to crescent. Its gravity makes the oceans ebb and flow. Earth's annual trip around the sun shifts temperatures from cold to warm. As life progressed on Earth, these rhythms became fixed in the chemistry of organisms. Studies have shown that humans and all other creatures possess **biological clocks** that keep things like body temperature, blood pressure, wakefulness, and other biological functions in tune with nature's patterns.

Resources on Earth, like **water** and important chemical compounds and elements, are fixed. They must cycle through the living and nonliving portions of the biosphere to keep its ecosystems functioning. **Oxygen**, **carbon**, and **nitrogen** are three elements crucial to the chemistry of life. Water is the universal solvent in which virtually all of these important reactions take place.

Look carefully at the water, oxygen, carbon, and nitrogen cycles illustrated below and answer the following questions.

1. What three processes must happen to water as it cycles in the biosphere?

   _____   _____   _____

2. Describe the roles of producers and consumers in the cycling of carbon dioxide and oxygen.

   _____

   _____

3. In what way are bacteria and fungi critical in cycling nitrogen in the biosphere?

   _____

Name: _____ Date: _____

Ecological Succession and Biomes

Your neighborhood may change as you grow up. People come and go. Others build new houses or start businesses. Old buildings may be torn down. In similar fashion, living communities change over time—a process called **ecological succession**. A forest fire, flood, or other disaster may reduce an area to bare soil or rock, but seeds take root, eventually animals return, and, given a sufficient amount of time, new communities arise. These communities may be simple at first, including plant opportunists like grasses and animal pioneers like insects, spiders, and small birds or mammals. Eventually, in a given climate and habitat, a stable community forms that will remain intact for many years, called the **climax community**.

Worldwide, environments with similar climates and ecological communities produce a relatively small number of community types called **biomes**. Cold and dry conditions form tundra biomes where the producers are often grasses, lichens, and other hardy plants consumed by grazing animals like caribou and visited by migrants like ducks and geese. **Conifer forests** claim somewhat wetter areas in high latitudes, while **deciduous forests**, where the trees annually shed their leaves, live at mid-latitudes. In the warm tropics, where 200 cm of rain may fall in a year, **tropical forests** thrive. **Grasslands** form in areas of moderate temperatures with an annual rainfall of 25 to 75 cm per year. Exceedingly hot and dry conditions with less than 25 cm of water per year generate **desert** biomes. Distinct **freshwater** and **marine** biomes form in the world's lakes and oceans with **estuary** communities forming where fresh and salt waters mix.

1. What is ecological succession? _____

   _____

2. Name six land biomes.

   _____   _____   _____

   _____

   _____

3. In what biome do you live?

   _____

   On your own paper, list five members from each kingdom of organisms that live within your biome.

   Legend:
   - Polar Ice
   - Tundra
   - Desert
   - Grassland
   - Tropical rain forest
   - Deciduous forest
   - Coniferous forest

Name: _____ Date: _____

Conservation and Biodiversity

Our third president, Thomas Jefferson, was also an amateur scientist. In 1796, he was sent three enormous claws found in a cave in West Virginia. At the time, Jefferson and others thought that huge animals possessing such claws might still live in unexplored parts of North America, because most people thought the animals and plants alive then had always existed. In fact, the fossil bones of dinosaurs and many other long-dead creatures show that 99% of Earth's life forms no longer exist. The process whereby entire species die is called **extinction.** Many species have become extinct since Jefferson's day, like the passenger pigeons that could fill the skies for days during their migrations.

A certain amount of extinction is a normal process. Die-offs called **mass extinction events** may result from rare events like the collision of Earth with large hunks of rock called **asteroids**. Such an event may have pushed dinosaurs to extinction. A great flood that covered the earth could have been another such event.

Today it appears that human beings are the cause of a major new extinction event. Sometimes they have caused extinctions by intentionally killing animals like the passenger pigeon. Other times, especially now, humans inadvertently cause extinctions because they use up habitats once available for other creatures. From 1950 to the year 2000, human populations increased from 2.5 billion to 6 billion people—more people than have ever existed in the past!

When the number and kinds of living things decrease, scientists call this a loss of **biodiversity**. Loss of biodiversity is like having a tool kit with an ever-decreasing number of tools. The fewer kinds of organisms available to recycle oxygen, carbon, nitrogen, and water, the less able living communities are to maintain the biosphere, just as an empty tool kit makes it impossible to fix a car or broken plumbing.

The attempt to save habitats, reduce pollution by human activity, prevent harvesting of some species, and preserve fresh water supplies is called **conservation**.

APPLY:

1. List six organisms that are now extinct.

   _____ _____ _____

   _____ _____ _____

   How many of these have become extinct in the last 50 years? _____

2. Look up the word *pollution* in the dictionary and write down the definition.

   _____

   List five possible sources of pollution produced in your town.

   _____ _____ _____

   _____ _____

3. What is *biodiversity*? _____

   Why is it important to maintain biodiversity in communities?

   _____

   _____

Name: _____ Date: _____

Part 1: Patterns in the Living World: Putting It All Together

CONTENT REVIEW

1. Modern classification systems for living things depend on looking at similarities in

    _____.

2. The two-part naming system devised by Carolus Linnaeus is called _____

    _____. The first part of the creature's scientific name is its

    _____. The second part is its _____.

3. The five kingdoms of living things that exist today ...

    A. have existed since the earth was created.

    B. are the archaea, fungi, plants, animals, and protists.

    C. represent the diversity of life.

    D. each have a very different genetic code.

4. T or F? Monerans have their genetic material contained within a cellular organelle called

    the nucleus.

5. If someone said they had found a basidiomycete in the woods last night, you know they

    found a member of the kingdom _____.

6. T or F? A lichen is an example of symbiosis.

7. Vascular plants have special tissues for conducting _____.

8. Living things have internal _____ _____ that

    help keep them in tune with nature's rhythms and cycles.

9. A tundra is a type of land biome that develops in parts of the world that are

    _____ and _____.

10. T or F? Extinction is a rare event in Earth's history.

Name: _____ Date: _____

Part 1: Patterns in the Living World: Putting It All Together (cont.)

CONCEPT REVIEW

1. T   or   F? Rapid human population growth has contributed to the increase in the normal rate of extinction on Earth.

2. If a conifer forest in Canada burned to the ground, in five years ...

   A. a deciduous forest would probably take its place.

   B. a pioneer community would be well-established.

   C. a mature climax community of conifers would have returned.

   D. no ecological succession is likely to have occurred.

3. A loss of soil microbes responsible for decomposition would especially disrupt the _____ cycle.

4. T   or   F? It would be reasonable to say that there are many more producers in a community than second-order consumers.

5. T   or   F? Looking at the diagram of the animal family tree on page 8, it is obvious that vertebrates are a superior form of life.

6. The kingdom that gets the prize for the most heterotrophic organisms is _____.

7. Viruses ...

   A. have an uncertain place in the classification of life.

   B. are certainly members of the moneran kingdom.

   C. sometimes are autotrophs.

   D. have a fundamentally different kind of genetic chemistry.

8. Arrange the following classification group names in increasing size from left to right:

   phylum   order   kingdom   species   class   family   genus

   A. _____   B. _____   C. _____

   D. _____   E. _____   F. _____

   G. _____

Part 2: Energy Flow in Living Systems: What Energizes Living Things?

All living things constantly consume energy in order to grow and reproduce. It's not surprising that life has developed on a rock (Earth) circling a very large source of energy (the sun). The sun provides most of the energy today for the living creatures with which we are most familiar. A few other sources exist that were more important early in our planet's history. For example, acid-loving monerans among the archaea can use the element sulfur to turn carbon dioxide into biologically useful compounds. While these creatures thrive in extreme heat, to them oxygen is a poison. They would have loved the conditions on the young Earth.

Many years ago, certain moneran cells acquired the trick of trapping light energy from the sun to make sugars. Oxygen was a waste by-product. As oxygen accumulated in the atmosphere, archaeans retreated to places like hot springs (on land) and hot vents in the ocean. Some methane producers live in termites and the guts of cows, returning carbon to the biosphere in the form of methane (CH_4).

So green plants and other producers are the first hogs to eat at the sun's energy trough. They get the most. When animals eat plants, some energy is lost as heat; the rest can be used for growth and reproduction. This happens all the way up the food chain. A kind of energy pyramid results. (See figure below.)

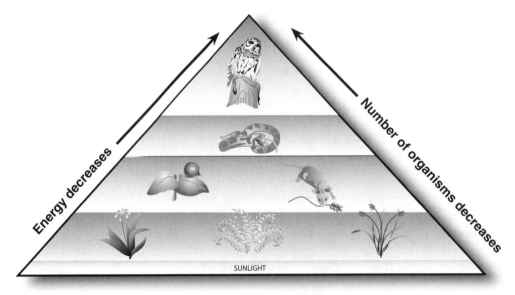

Energy pyramid

All plants aren't eaten, however. The energy included in much plant substance (**biomass**) either flows through decomposers or gets temporarily stored in so-called **fossil fuels** like coal and oil—which is nothing more than compressed or liquefied plant and animal biomass. Much of the coal and oil used today by humans was deposited during a particularly warm and wet time many years ago when forests covered the world. Humans have also learned to use the heat energy of the cooling Earth (**geothermal energy**) and the energy used to hold the atomic building blocks of matter together (**nuclear energy**).

16

Looking at Life in the Past

Fossils provide a glimpse of life during Earth's past. The roots of the modern five kingdoms of living things go back to this ancient time period. The creatures of this period had already been carrying on the complex chemistry of life.

The rock record and other evidence show that early Earth was different from today. Noxious gases like methane, hydrogen sulfide, ammonia, and hydrogen cyanide most likely made up a significant part of its atmosphere.

Today we know that all living things are made up of small subunits called **cells**. Living things **move**, even if it is the subtle motions of plants and fungi. Living things eat, grow, and **excrete wastes**. They **respond to stimuli** in their environments, **reproduce** when at all possible, and eventually **die**. To accomplish these actions, living creatures need energy, food and water, space, and a suitable temperature in which chemical activities can function.

As life formed, its activities eventually transformed the earth. The warm, wet, oxygenated atmosphere of today's Earth resulted from the organized world of the five kingdoms.

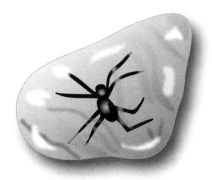

Spider trapped in amber

Clypeaster **in sand**

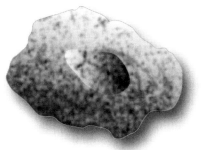

Impression of beetle in tar and sand

Ammonite shell replaced by minerals

Leaf in mudstone

Different types of fossils

Cellular Organization and Fundamental Chemistries

To build the molecules of life, you mostly need the elements of **c**arbon, **h**ydrogen, **o**xygen, and **n**itrogen—just remember: CHON! Combine CHON atoms in one way to form **carbohydrates**—sugars and starches. Combine the same atoms in a slightly different way and you can make **fats** (solid at room temperature) and **oils** (liquid at room temperature). For building things like muscle, you need **protein**, built from CHON along with **s**ulfur and a few other elements now and then. Proteins are made from subunits called **amino acids**. One entire class of proteins called **enzymes** helps to speed up or **catalyze** important chemical reactions. To make hereditary chemicals of life, combine CHONS with some phosphorus to make **nucleic acids**. **Ribonucleic acid (RNA)** and **deoxyribonucleic acid (DNA)** are both nucleic acids created with different sugar subunits—ribose and deoxyribose sugars, respectively.

Living things make all their chemical requirements within subunits called **cells**. Cells are basic to the structure and function of living things. Living cells come only from the reproduction of existing cells. These three statements make up what scientists describe as the **cell theory of life**.

The illustrations below show typical plant and animal cells and the amazing parts of which they are composed.

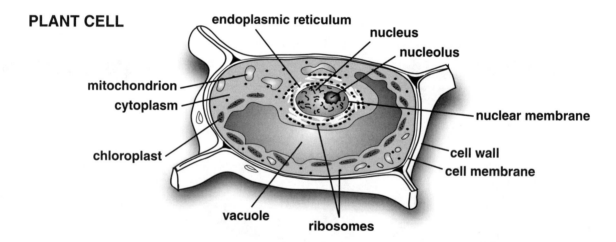

PLANT CELL

endoplasmic reticulum · nucleus · nucleolus · mitochondrion · cytoplasm · nuclear membrane · chloroplast · cell wall · cell membrane · vacuole · ribosomes

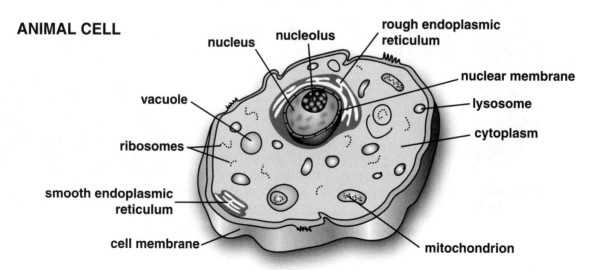

ANIMAL CELL

nucleus · nucleolus · rough endoplasmic reticulum · vacuole · nuclear membrane · lysosome · ribosomes · cytoplasm · smooth endoplasmic reticulum · cell membrane · mitochondrion

Critical Chemistry: Photosynthesis and Respiration

Early cells converted sugars to alcohol and carbon dioxide in a process called **fermentation**. Some early monerans developed pigments called **chlorophyll** that were able to trap the energy of light and make that energy available for making those tasty carbohydrates called **sugars**. This process of **photosynthesis** requires a source of carbon—provided in the early atmosphere, as today, by carbon dioxide—and a source of hydrogen. In the beginning, this hydrogen came from compounds like hydrogen sulfide (the cause of the smell of rotten eggs), which was readily available.

Moneran photosynthesis: carbon dioxide + hydrogen sulfide + water (in the presence of light and chlorophyll) yields sugar + sulfur, or $4\ CO_2 + 2\ H_2S + 4\ H_2O \xrightarrow{\text{light energy + bacterial chlorophyll}}$ $4\ CH_2O + 2\ H_2SO_4$.

During Earth's Precambrian Era, monerans like the modern creatures called *Nostoc* busily made their sugars with a form of photosynthesis still used by all modern plants. The hydrogen donor became water, and the "waste product" of the creation is oxygen!

Green plant photosynthesis: carbon dioxide + water (in the presence of light and bacterial chlorophyll) yields sugar + oxygen, or $6\ CO_2 + 6\ H_2O \xrightarrow{\text{chlorophyll a}} C_6H_{12}O_6 + 6\ O_2$.

Oxygen concentrations built up in the oceans, then began "leaking" into the atmosphere. Oxygen was a poison for early life, so living things faced their first pollution problem.

Consumer monerans used all the excess oxygen molecules to use food more efficiently in a process called **respiration**. As in fermentation, sugar gets changed to a compound called pyruvate, but pyruvate now enters a complex set of reactions called the **citric acid cycle** that yields as an end-product carbon dioxide, water, and sixteen times more energy than fermentation in the form of a compound called **ATP**. Sugar + oxygen yields carbon dioxide + water + energy, or $C_6H_{12}O_6 + 6\ O_2 \longrightarrow 6\ CO_2 + 6\ H_2O$ + energy (ATP). The citric acid cycle reactions occur in the cell organelles called **mitochondria**.

Notice how photosynthesis requires carbon dioxide to work and produces sugars with oxygen as a by-product. Both producers and consumers benefit. Realize, too, that producers must use the process of respiration to build and grow their own tissues. Land plants acquire carbon dioxide from the air through openings in their leaves called **stomata**. Water is drawn in by roots and rises within vascular tissue in the stems and leaves. Green plant photosynthesis occurs in the organelles called **chloroplasts**.

Photosynthesis and respiration appear to be ancient examples of symbiosis between the moneran, plant, and animal kingdoms.

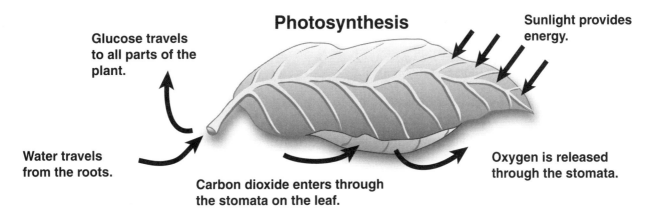

Photosynthesis

Glucose travels to all parts of the plant.

Sunlight provides energy.

Water travels from the roots.

Carbon dioxide enters through the stomata on the leaf.

Oxygen is released through the stomata.

Mitosis: Cellular Reproduction

 One might think that a single cell could grow indefinitely like some sort of blob monster from a science fiction movie, but cells can only grow so big before transporting food, water, and oxygen becomes a problem. Cells must divide in order for large creatures to develop. The process of cell division is called **mitosis**. The stages or phases of mitosis are quite similar in all the living kingdoms as seen below.

(1) **Interphase:** The complex of nucleic acids and protein that make up the chromosomes in the nucleus are loosely coiled in threads of **chromatin**. Toward the end of interphase, this chromatin duplicates itself. The copies are held together at one point along their length by a structure called the **centromere**. Each copy is now called a **chromatid**. Animal cells have two small structures outside the nucleus called **centrioles** that are involved in mitosis.

(2) **Prophase:** The chromatids thicken and begin to become distinct. The centrioles in animal cells begin to move to opposite ends of the nucleus, and a structure called the **spindle** begins to form between them. Plant cells form a spindle without the centrioles. The nuclear membrane begins to break down and the nucleolus, if present, disappears.

(3) **Metaphase:** The chromosomes attach to the spindle in a line near the center of the cell.

(4) **Anaphase:** The centromere splits and the chromatids, now full-fledged chromosomes, begin to pull apart toward opposite centrioles.

(5) **Telophase:** New nuclear membranes begin to form around the duplicated chromosomes. The chromosomes uncoil, and the nucleolus reappears in each new cell. Centrioles replicate.

(6) **Cytokinesis:** The cytoplasm between new cells is pinched apart, and a cell membrane reforms at the junction.

1. Interphase	2. Prophase	3. Metaphase	4. Anaphase	5. Telophase

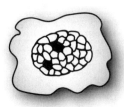 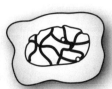   

Cell division occurs millions of times as organisms grow and as they need to repair or replace damaged tissues.

Name: _____ Date: _____

Part 2: Energy Flow in Living Systems: Putting It All Together

CONTENT REVIEW

1. T or F? First-order consumers trap most of the energy available in sunlight.

2. All living creatures require _____, _____, _____, _____, and a fairly narrow range of _____ for chemical reactions to occur.

3. Plant cells possess _____ and _____, two structures not found in animal cells.

4. Circle the letter of the true statement:

    A. Fermentation yields more energy than respiration.

    B. Moneran photosynthesis produces oxygen as a by-product.

    C. Green plant photosynthesis requires CO_2 and H_2O.

    D. Chlorophyll is a chemical in the citric acid cycle.

5. T or F? During anaphase in the process of cell division, the chromatids begin to pull apart.

CONCEPT REVIEW

1. T or F? Centrioles don't seem to be critical to the formation of spindles during mitosis in all organisms.

2. Under what conditions does fermentation work better than respiration for acquiring energy? _____

   _____

3. What do muscles and enzymes have in common? _____

   _____

4. T or F? It's not likely that life could arise on Mars because there is no free oxygen in its atmosphere.

5. Which of the following energy sources is *least* likely to be available in 1,000 years?

   Circle one.   A. Solar   B. Oil   C. Geothermal   D. Nuclear

Name: _____ Date: _____

Part 3: The Human Animal and Levels of Organization: Humans' Place in Nature

Where do humans fit within the natural world? We sometimes look at our mental skills—especially our abilities to communicate through speech, to reason, to be aware of our own existence and eventual death, have spiritual connections—and consider ourselves something above and beyond the rest of the living world.

Linnaeus recognized the structural similarity of humans to other mobile heterotrophs (animals). Here is our full classification "address":

Kingdom: Animalia
Phylum: Chordata (animals with backbones called **vertebrates**)
Class: Mammalia (vertebrates with hair, milk glands for feeding their young, and that give birth to live young)
Order: Primate (tree-living mammals with five fingers, five toes, and collarbones, or clavicles)
Family: Hominidae (ground-living primates with large heads that walk upright and have teeth adapted for a varied diet. Other living great apes, like gorillas, chimps, and orangutans, belong in the family Pongidae.)
Genus: Homo (Hominids are usually defined by a certain brain size and tooth characteristics. No other non-human members of this genus live today.)
Species: *sapien* (Homo the wise)

The recent ability to sequence the entire **genome** (gene sequence) of humans and chimps has shown that humans differ in only 1% of their genes from chimpanzees. Of course, 50% of human genes are the same as those found in bananas. Life is conservative. We'll soon take a detailed look at the human body plan, and in the process, learn a lot about life in general.

1. T or F? Human beings are fundamentally different from other animals on Earth.

2. Human beings and chimpanzees both belong to the order _____.

3. No living creatures alive today belong to the genus _____ except human beings.

4. Humans and bananas probably share which of the following?

    A. The same chemical reactions for respiration

    B. The same chloroplast chemistry

    C. The same kind of body support structure

    D. All of the above

Levels of Organization

Human bodies, like those of other creatures, are composed of **cells**. The various cells look quite different depending on the function they perform. Cells with similar functions unite to form specialized **tissues**. The body contains four basic tissue types: **muscle**, **connective**, **nerve**, and **epithelial**.

Muscle tissue contracts in various ways to move body parts. **Skeletal muscle** allows quick motion, **smooth muscle** allows for slow, rhythmic motion, like that needed for digestion, and **cardiac muscle** performs the special, continuous contractions of the heart.

Connective tissue provides support and includes things like bone, blood, and fat. **Nerve tissue** transmits messages from the brain to all parts of the body and back again. **Epithelial tissue** provides a protective outer coating in the form of skin.

Tissues are further organized into specific organs like the heart, stomach, brain, eye, and skin, which are all composed of more than one tissue type. Organs, in turn, work together as **organ systems** to perform life's necessary tasks. The human body contains the following organ systems:

- **Skeletal:** Provides protection, support, slow movement, stores minerals, and creates blood cells.
- **Muscular:** Works with the skeletal system to provide movement.
- **Digestive:** Breaks down food; absorbs nutrients.
- **Circulatory:** Transports necessary materials and plays a role in the immune response.
- **Respiratory:** Provides for gas exchange between air and the body.
- **Excretory:** Removes solid and liquid wastes.
- **Nervous:** Senses things in the environment and controls bodily activities.
- **Endocrine:** Helps regulate metabolism, reproduction, and other functions.
- **Reproductive:** Performs reproductive activities and behavior.
- **Immune:** Controls immune responses to disease-causing invaders.
- **Integumentary:** (skin) Protects; regulates temperature and water loss.

All multicellular organisms function at four progressively more complex **levels of organization**—the cellular, tissue, organ, and organ system levels—which all act in harmony together.

Spinal cord (tissue)

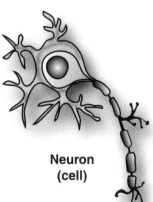

Neuron (cell)

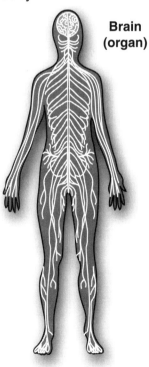

Brain (organ)

Nervous system (organ system)

Skeletal and Muscular Systems

The human skeletal system with its 206 bones performs five important functions: it provides **shape** and **support**, allows **movement**, **protects** tissues and organs, **stores** certain materials, and **produces blood cells** in bone marrow. The muscular system provides muscles of three types—skeletal, smooth, and cardiac—to assist in moving the body, to process food, and to keep the heart pumping, respectively. Look carefully at the following illustration to see these systems' important parts and features.

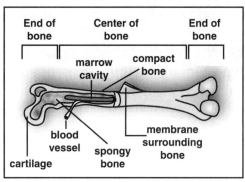

End of bone   Center of bone   End of bone

marrow cavity
compact bone
blood vessel
spongy bone
membrane surrounding bone
cartilage

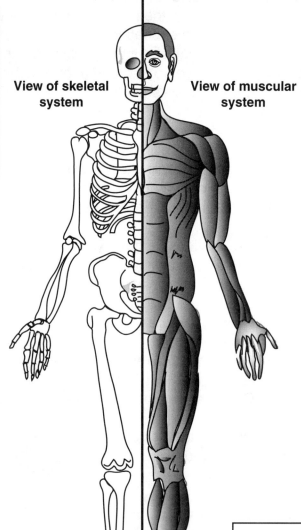

View of skeletal system   View of muscular system

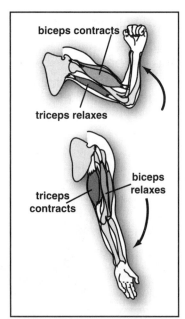

biceps contracts
triceps relaxes

triceps contracts
biceps relaxes

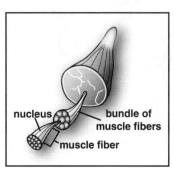

nucleus
bundle of muscle fibers
muscle fiber

Ligament

Digestive System

The human digestive system does an admirable job of breaking down food into simpler substances the body can use to maintain itself and perform. The usable portion of things we eat are called **nutrients** and include **proteins**, **carbohydrates**, **fats**, **vitamins**, **minerals**, and **water**. (See page 18.)

Find the following parts of the digestive system in the illustration below:

1. **Mouth:** Mushes up food with the action of the teeth; secretes saliva, which contains **ptyalin**, an **enzyme** that changes some starches into sugars.
2. **Esophagus:** Moves food to the stomach with the help of smooth muscles, which contract rhythmically in a process called **peristalsis**.
3. **Stomach:** Breaks food apart through muscular action and secretes digestive juices that contain the enzyme **pepsin**, **hydrochloric acid** (**HCl**), and mucus. Pepsin and HCl act together to help break down proteins, like those found in meat.
4. **Small intestine:** Most digestion occurs here. The enzymes **lactase**, **maltase**, and **sucrase** turn complex sugars into simple sugars. **Peptidase** converts simple proteins to amino acids. **Lipase** breaks up fats into **fatty acids** and **glycerol**. **Bile**, which is produced in the liver and stored in the gall bladder, also breaks up fats. **Pancreatic juice** from the **pancreas** contains **amylase**, **trypsin**, and **lipase,** which help break down starches, proteins, and fats, respectively. Nutrients are absorbed by finger-like projections called **villi** and pass into the blood for transport.
5. **Large intestine:** Reabsorbs excess water. Resident bacteria make vitamin K and two B vitamins. The **rectum** temporarily stores undigested waste material before ejection from the **anus**.

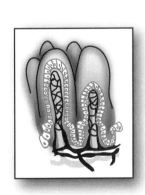

INSET: Nutrients are passed into the blood by the villi in the small intestine.

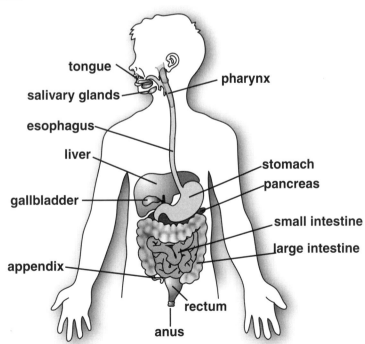

Circulatory System

The **arteries** and **veins** of the human circulatory system, like interstate highways, provide pathways for moving things around. **Blood** transports food and oxygen to the body's cells, and it picks up carbon dioxide and other wastes for disposal. The circulatory system also transports supplies for the body's defense and coordination.

The **heart**, a central pumping station, cycles blood back and forth to the lungs for gas exchange and to all parts of the body and back for transport of other material. Small tubes one cell thick called **capillaries** connect outgoing arteries and incoming veins.

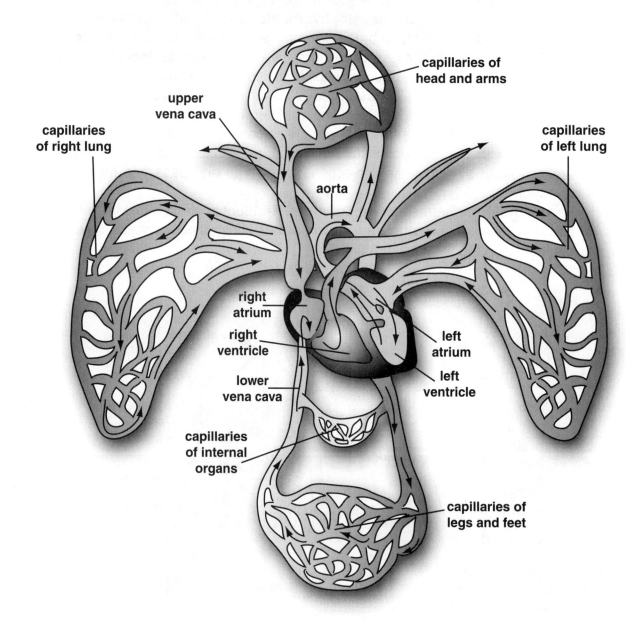

Circulatory System (cont.)

The liquid blood plasma is 90% water and 10% sugars, fats, salts, gases, and plasma proteins. Plasma proteins include water regulators, antibodies (for defense), and blood-clotting agents (in case the plumbing breaks). Plasma also contains digested food, hormones (chemical messengers), and waste products.

The solid portion of blood includes **red cells**, **white cells**, and cell fragments called **platelets**. Red cells, produced in bone marrow, have no nucleus and survive about 120 days. They contain **hemoglobin**, which transports oxygen and carbon dioxide. White cells do possess nuclei. Some may live for years, and they come in several varieties. They clean up old red cells and engulf invading pathogens. Platelets break open at the site of a wound and release **fibrin**, a fibrous clotting protein that traps blood solids to create a scab until the body can replace ruptured epithelium (skin).

Blood contains unique proteins, simply labeled **A** and **B**, and 18 other **Rh proteins**. People can fall into the following **blood groups**: **A** (just the A protein); **B** (just the B protein); **AB** (they have both); or **O** (they have neither). In addition, a person is designated **+** if they have any Rh proteins and **−** if they have none. If people need to have blood replaced because of injury, blood types must be matched carefully—otherwise, fatal blood clotting will occur.

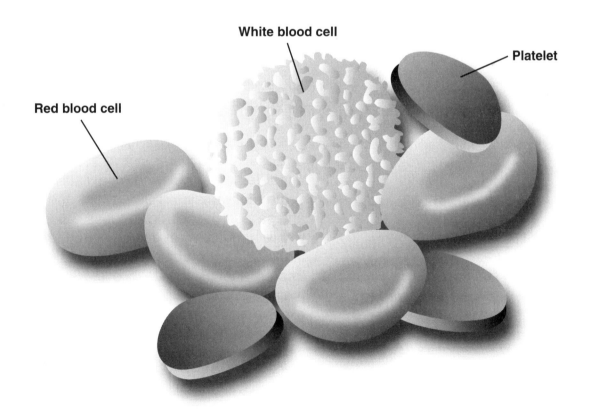

White blood cell

Platelet

Red blood cell

27

Respiration and Excretion

The **respiratory system** extracts oxygen from the air we breathe and removes carbon dioxide and excess water from blood. Incoming air gets warmed up in the **nasal cavity**, and **mucus** helps filter out dust and bacteria. Lowering the muscular **diaphragm** draws air into the **lungs** through the **trachea** and **bronchial tubes** where gases are exchanged in grape-like bunches of **alveoli** well-served with **capillaries**. Raising the diaphragm expels waste-laden air out the same passages.

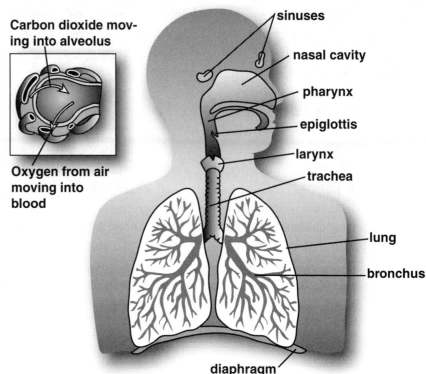

Carbon dioxide moving into alveolus

Oxygen from air moving into blood

sinuses
nasal cavity
pharynx
epiglottis
larynx
trachea
lung
bronchus
diaphragm

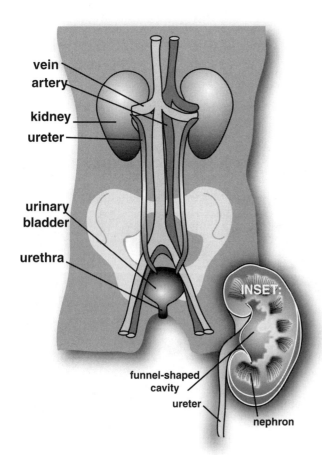

vein
artery
kidney
ureter
urinary bladder
urethra
INSET
funnel-shaped cavity
ureter
nephron

The **excretory system** removes water and salts, carbon dioxide, and **urea**, a nitrogen compound. The **kidneys** filter wastes from the blood in specialized tubules called **nephrons**. In the process, they reabsorb important nutrients, salts, and water in a structure called the **capsule**, which is filled with capillaries. The **urine** that remains is 96% water and 4% urea and salts. It passes down tubes called **ureters** where about a quart can be stored temporarily in the **urinary bladder** before being eliminated through the **urethra**. While the kidney is the main organ of this system, the **liver** removes excess amino acids from protein breakdown and converts the hemoglobin of dead red blood cells into bile. It also breaks down bacterial invaders. The **skin**, another important excretory organ, expels salts, urea, and excess water through sweat glands.

Nervous and Endocrine Systems

The **nervous** and **endocrine systems** work together (along with the circulatory system) as a "communications central." The nervous system is composed of specialized cells called **neurons**, which come in three varieties: **sensory neurons**, **interneurons**, and **motor neurons**. Sensory neurons transmit signals from specialized environmental receptors (eyes, ears, skin, nose, and tongue) to the interneurons of the **brain** and **spinal cord** for analysis. These organs commit the body to action by sending messages through motor neurons to muscles or **glands** (part of the endocrine system). Muscles and glands are called **effectors**.

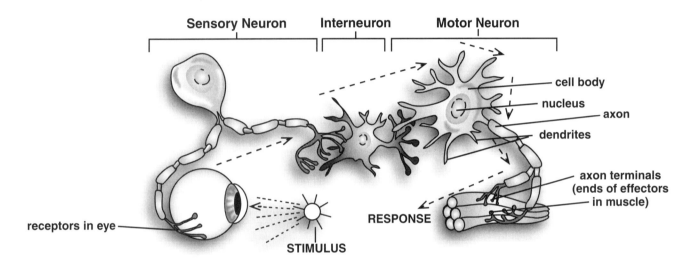

The **central nervous system** (CNS) consists of the brain and spinal cord. The brain consists of the **cerebrum** (site of intelligence, judgment, and voluntary action), the **cerebellum** (site of muscle coordination and balance), and the **medulla** (the site of involuntary "housekeeping") or **autonomic** activities like maintaining heartbeat, breathing, and blood pressure. The spinal cord handles involuntary **reflexes** that must occur without deliberate thought. The **peripheral nervous system** (PNS) branches from the CNS to all of the various parts of the body. (See the illustration on page 23.)

The **endocrine system** consists of a series of glands that release chemical messengers called **hormones**. Find the glands in the figure at the right, and then look at the following chart to see what each gland does in the body.

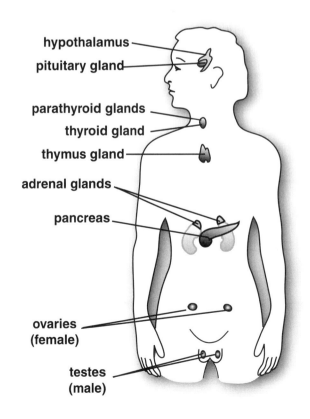

29

Nervous and Endocrine Systems (cont.)

GLAND	HORMONE(S)	FUNCTION
Hypothalamus	Regulatory factors	Regulates other glands
Pituitary (front)	Human growth hormone Gonadatropic hormone Lactogenic hormone Thyrotropic hormone Adrenocorticotropic hormone (ACTH)	Stimulates body/skeletal growth Development of sexual organs Stimulates milk production Aids functions of thyroid
Pituitary (back)	Oxytocin Vasopressin	Regulates blood pressure; stimulates muscles used during childbirth Regulates water reabsorption in kidneys
Thymus	Thymosin	Regulates aspects of immune systems
Thyroid	Thyroxine Calcitonin	Increases rate of metabolism Maintains calcium and potassium in blood
Parathyroids	Parathyroid hormone	Regulates calcium and potassium in blood
Adrenals (inner)	Adrenaline	Increases heart rate; elevates blood pressure; raises blood sugar; increases breathing rate; decreases digestion
Adrenals (outer)	Mineralocorticoids Glucocorticoids— cortisone	Salt and water balance Breaks down proteins; aids fat breakdown; promotes increase in blood sugar Supplements sex hormones produced by sex glands; promotes sexual characteristics
Pancreas	Insulin Glucagon	Regulates sugar breakdown and storage; decreases blood sugar levels Increases blood sugar levels
Ovaries	Estrogen Progesterone	Female secondary sexual traits Promotes growth of uterine lining
Testes	Testosterone	Male secondary sexual traits

Name: _____ Date: _____

Diseases: Infectious or Not?

 We are all familiar with **infectious diseases**—the kind of illnesses that can pass from person to person. These kinds of diseases are caused by tiny **microorganisms**, including bacteria, protoctists, fungi, and viruses. Sometimes people label all microorganisms as "bad" and the cause of disease, but those forms are a minority and tend to specialize in a fairly narrow range of hosts. Human beings are subject to their share of these.

Microorganisms may cause illness in several ways: (1) By simply growing out of control and disrupting normal function—like the bacteria that cause tuberculosis (TB) that grow in lung tissue until the lung's owner can't breathe properly. (2) By producing poisons or **toxins** that damage organs or tissues—like the salmonella bacteria responsible for food poisoning. (3) By destroying cells and tissues of their host through their own reproduction. This is the style of viruses like those that cause colds and flu that co-opt the cell machinery of their host to make more virus particles.

Microorganisms can move from person to person in the 5,000 or so droplets of moisture produced in every sneeze or cough, through shaking hands or touching surfaces touched by a sick person, through waste water, or through sexual contact in the case of diseases like gonorrhea and syphilis. Sometimes diseases need an intermediate host or **vector**, like a tick or a mosquito. Ticks spread Lyme disease. Mosquitoes carry malaria, yellow fever, and West Nile Virus.

Infectious diseases used to be the major cause of illness and death among humans. Since sanitation, health care, and diet have improved, many **non-infectious** diseases have become important. Cancer is runaway cell growth that may be caused by random mutations in a cell's DNA or mutations caused by certain chemicals in the environment (**carcinogens**). **Diabetes mellitus**, a disease that can cause severe sugar regulation problems, and **coronary heart disease** that leads to heart attacks, can have both genetic and environmental components. **Scurvy**, caused by a lack of vitamin C in the diet, is one of several **vitamin deficiency diseases**. Poor diet and stress can make people more susceptible to both infectious and non-infectious diseases.

APPLY:

1. In what three ways can microorganisms cause disease?

    A. _____

    B. _____

    C. _____

2. Washing your hands with soap and water can be the most effective single way to avoid transmitting disease. Why? Answer on another sheet of paper.

3. Three non-infectious diseases are _____, _____, and _____.

The Immune System: The Body Fights Back

The body fights diseases with three main lines of defense. **First-line defenses** include skin, mucus, saliva (spit), and stomach acid. Quit laughing! Skin, as thin and soft as it seems, keeps out a wide range of microbial invaders. Mucus, mostly of the nose variety, globs them up so that you can blow or drip them out. If microbes are swallowed, all of that hydrochloric acid in your stomach goes to work on them. Saliva, or spit, also has chemicals that microbes don't like.

Second-line defenses include an array of white blood cells. When invaders attack your body's cells and tissues, one set of white cells in the blood moves into infected tissues and gobbles up the offending microbes. This action attracts more white cell types, and the "battlefield" area becomes red, swollen, and warm. This is called the **inflammatory response**. The body also produces a substance called **interferon** that "interferes" with viral reproduction.

Third-line defenses include **antibodies**, which are special proteins that either float freely in the blood or attach themselves to white cells. Foreign creatures in your body (technically called **antigens**) stimulate the production of antibodies that exactly match these invaders and stick to their surfaces in such a way that they have trouble attaching to healthy cells and also are more easily

A cut in the skin healing over with a scab

swallowed by **phagocytic** white blood cells. White cells called **T-cells** produced in the thymus gland alert white **B-cells** produced in bone marrow to create antibodies. The first time you get sick with something like measles, you feel ill because it takes time for this process to occur. But for diseases like the measles, the body can rally antibodies right away when exposed again, so you don't get sick from the measles a second time.

Catching a disease that causes you to make antibodies or getting vaccinated with a weakened strain of a disease for the same purpose results in **active immunity**—immunity created by your body. Getting injected with antibodies produced by other animals or getting antibodies from your mother in the womb is an example of **passive immunity**. The latter kind is temporary.

When the immune system becomes hypersensitive to certain substances (**allergens**) in the environment, the body releases **histamines** that cause watery eyes, running nose, and sneezing. **Allergies** of this sort are often treated with **antihistamines**.

AIDS, or acquired immune deficiency syndrome, results when a virus (**HIV**, or human immunodeficiency virus) attacks and destroys T-cells. This weakens the victim's immune system, and he or she dies from secondary infections. AIDS can only be transmitted through blood contaminated with HIV, such as through an open cut or a needle stick, and during the exchange of fluids during sex. Currently, drugs can slow, but not cure, AIDS.

Name: _____ Date: _____

Part 3: The Human Animal and Levels of Organization: Putting It All Together

CONTENT REVIEW

1. T or F? There are other creatures alive today on Earth that are classified in the same family as human beings.

2. Multicellular organisms function at four levels of organization, which are: _____, _____, _____, and _____.

3. _____ hold bones together while _____ connect muscle to bones.

4. T or F? Most digestion of nutrients occurs in the stomach.

5. The solid portion of blood contains ...

    A. red cells, white cells, enzymes, and proteins.

    B. red cells, white cells, and platelets.

    C. red cells, hemoglobin, and white cells.

    D. red cells, white cells, and Rh proteins.

6. T or F? The skin is an important excretory organ.

7. The bronchial tubes in the lungs end in tiny, grape-like structures called _____, where gas exchange occurs.

8. The central nervous system consists of the _____ and _____.

9. The glands of the endocrine systems produce messenger chemicals called _____.

10. Cancer is a kind of (infectious / non-infectious) disease. (Circle the correct answer.)

11. T or F? A second line of defense for the body is mucus.

Name: _____ Date: _____

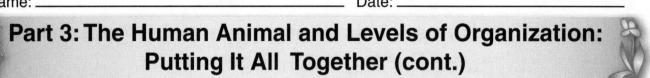

Part 3: The Human Animal and Levels of Organization: Putting It All Together (cont.)

CONTENT REVIEW

1. If someone has AIDS, you can catch it ...

    A. by shaking hands with him.

    B. by drinking from the same cup he used.

    C. by getting his blood in an open wound of yours.

    D. if he coughs in your face.

2. T or F? Some infectious diseases can be controlled by eliminating their intermediate vector.

3. If a person's cerebellum were damaged, you would expect ...

    A. his coordination would be affected.

    B. his judgment would be impaired.

    C. his reflexes would be slowed.

    D. he might have trouble breathing.

4. How can a person continue to function normally when he has a kidney removed?

    _____

5. If someone had a genetic disease where he couldn't produce fibrin, what problems would he have? _____

6. If someone has a gall bladder removed, he might have trouble digesting _____.

7. How would bone marrow cancer have an impact on the circulatory system?

    _____

8. An eye is an example of the _____ level of organization.

Part 4: Descent and Change: Methods of Reproduction and Meiosis

Eating, growing, competing, and everything else living things do all serve the prime motivation to reproduce. The ability of the nucleic acids, RNA and DNA, to reproduce themselves precisely (See page 41.) marked those chemicals as fundamental to reproduction and heredity.

The simplest independent organisms exist at the cellular level of organization. The mechanism of **mitosis** (See page 20.) provides a way for cells to divide in such a way that cell contents and genetic information are divided equally between daughter cells. Moneran cells like bacteria divide by mitosis in a process called **fission**, a type of **asexual reproduction**. In bad times, bacteria may also form **spores**—essentially cells with a protective coating and slowed metabolism—that can germinate into active cells when favorable conditions return. Bacteria can exchange genetic information with other cells, but the process is not linked to reproduction as it is in **sexual reproduction**.

A type of "reduction division" called **meiosis** results in sex cells containing half the normal amount of chromosomes and genetic information. These cells are called **gametes**. Large gametes are called **eggs**; small motile ones are called **sperm**.

Recall that in the phase of mitosis called metaphase, the chromosomes line up in the center of the cell. During meiosis, instead of lining up randomly, chromosomes line up in matched pairs. During the following anaphase, the centromeres don't divide when the chromosomes pull apart, resulting in half the number of chromosomes in each daughter cell. Each daughter cell enters a new metaphase where the centromeres do split, pulling chromatids apart into new chromosomes. The result is a cluster of four gametes, each containing half the chromosomes of the original parent cell.

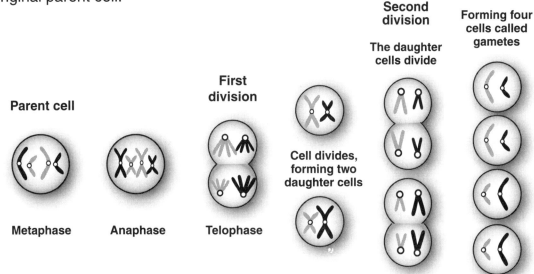

During egg production in humans and other mammals, three of the gametes during each meiosis shrink and die, leaving one huge egg cell with lots of nutrients in females. Males produce four sperm for each meiotic division, which develop long flagella to move them up the female reproductive tract. When egg and sperm unite to form a fertilized egg cell or **zygote**, the normal number of chromosomes for a given species is restored.

Patterns of Development: Animals

All animals start out as single cells that divide by mitosis to form a hollow ball of cells called a **blastula**. That ball begins to poke inward on one end, or invaginate, to form a **gastrula**. The young embryo now possesses two types of tissue: an outer **ectoderm** and an inner **endoderm**. In simple animals like sponges and coelenterates, this tube-within-a-tube plan is all there is. Food comes in and wastes exit through the same opening. More advanced animals like the frogs, dogs, insects, and clams with which we are familiar, develop a third tissue between the other two called the **mesoderm** from which muscles and other tissues form.

Also, the embryos of **vertebrates** (animals with backbones) and **invertebrates** (animals without backbones) show a fundamental difference: the opening that forms in the gastrula in vertebrates eventually becomes the anus; in invertebrates, that opening becomes the mouth.

One of the most successful groups of invertebrates are the insects. The first insects that appear in the fossil record are insects with a type of development called **incomplete metamorphosis**. The young insects, or **larvae**, look much like adults—and tend to feed on the same plants—but they don't have wings. Insects have external skeletons that can't expand much in size. In order to grow larger, an insect must shed or **molt** its old skeleton, expand while the skin is soft, and then harden that skin at the bigger size. During the last molt, the wings form.

Today 90% of insects develop with **complete metamorphosis**, a process where another developmental stage is added: the **pupa**. The egg develops into larvae that go through several molts, but the last molt is a sedentary phase called a pupa that is often an overwintering stage. Within the pupa, completely different insect genes express themselves so that when the adult emerges, it looks totally different from its larval forms. An example is a caterpillar turning into a butterfly. This kind of development apparently allowed insects to exploit different food plants at different life stages.

The earliest vertebrate embryos developed in water like those of frogs and salamanders today. Although these **amphibians** often live on dry land as adults, they must return to water to breed and lay eggs. **Reptiles** and **birds** lay eggs that maintain a watery environment within a shell and also provide additional food for embryonic development. Birds often protect and warm their eggs until they hatch. Humans and other **mammals** take the ultimate step in protecting their young by retaining the egg inside the body. The growing embryo feeds off the mother and is sheltered within her uterus.

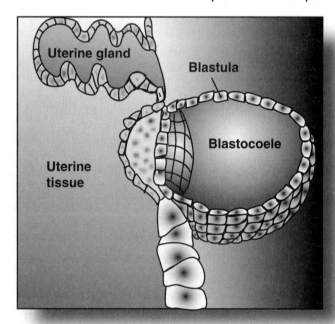

This early stage of human development is called a blastula.

Patterns of Development: Humans

The growth of a human fertilized egg cell from something the size of a grain of sand to a full-term baby in nine months staggers the imagination. The mass of the egg increases 2.4 billion times! The human **embryo** begins to divide as it passes down the mother's fallopian tube. When it reaches the uterus, it implants on its wall and forms two important structures: a protective, water-filled enclosure called the **amniotic sac** and a tissue called the **placenta** that develops from both the mother's and the embryo's tissue. The placenta handles the functions of nourishment, respiration, and excretion for the new human.

After eight weeks of development, the walnut-sized embryo is called a **fetus**. After three months, the heartbeat may be heard by the doctor, and the major internal organs have developed. By the end of the sixth month, the lungs begin to develop. During the final three months before birth, the lungs and other organs begin to change in a way that will prepare the fetus for life outside the womb. By the ninth month, the fetus can breathe, suck his thumb, swallow, blink, and perform other movements that will be needed when he is out in the world. The period from conception to birth is called a **pregnancy**.

The birth process begins with **labor**, a period where strong muscular contractions push the baby through the cervix and into the vagina. Labor can last two to 20 hours. The **delivery** expels the baby from the vagina. Crying makes the infant's lungs operational. The umbilical cord is cut and tied about five centimeters from the baby's abdomen. Further contractions remove the rich lining of the uterus along with the placenta, called the **afterbirth**.

Human development continues after birth in four stages: **infancy**, **childhood**, **adolescence**, and **adulthood**. Infancy lasts from birth to two years and sees a rapid increase in size and skills. By three months, infants can hold their heads up and reach for things—like your nose. By five months, they can grab hold of things; by seven months, they are crawling; and by ten to fourteen months, they are walking.

Childhood lasts from two to 13 years. Mental abilities increase, along with memory and coordination. Baby teeth fall out, to be followed by a permanent set, and the signature ability of humans to use language develops.

Adolescence begins with the onset of **puberty**—or development of the sexual organs—and lasts until about age 20. Women begin to menstruate on a monthly cycle, and men begin to produce sperm. A growth spurt occurs in females between 10–16 years and in males between 11–17 years.

During adulthood, fat moves from surface features, like the face, and the nose and ears may continue to grow. Aging begins around the age of 30, but becomes noticeable between the ages of 40–65 as the skin becomes less elastic, hair grays, and strength decreases. During this latter period, women experience **menopause** where menstruation ceases. Men continue to produce sperm, but in smaller quantities.

Patterns of Development: Plants

The plants called **algae** that live in fresh and salt water live in a medium that makes the exchange of sex cells pretty easy. They can float or swim their way to each other. When plants invaded dry land, they faced more severe problems of drying out. Still, the simplest plants, like mosses and liverworts are small enough—and they tend to live in moist environments—that their sex cells manage to reach each other.

As plants developed **vascular**, or water-conducting tissue, as well as roots and leaves, they tended to grow larger and became more successful at colonizing land, but that success came with the price of finding ways to make reproduction work in a hostile environment. Ferns solved the problem by alternating a large spore-producing or **sporophyte** generation with a small, and very moss-like **gametophyte** generation. Meiosis takes place in the spores so that each spore germinates into a tiny plant with only one set of chromosomes. This **haploid** generation makes male and female gametes that unite to form a **zygote**. The zygote grows into the familiar sporophyte or **diploid** plant with a complete set of paired chromosomes.

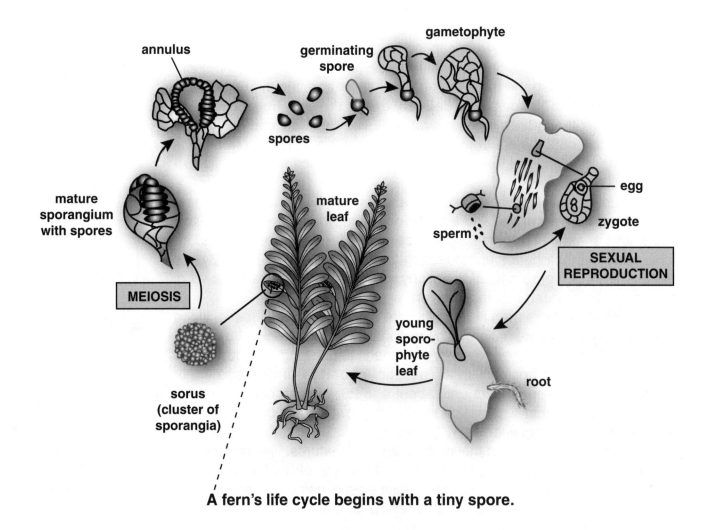

A fern's life cycle begins with a tiny spore.

Patterns of Development: Plants (cont.)

Eventually, plants retained the gametophyte generation within the sporophyte form to create little reproductive lifeboats called **seeds**. In some plants, like pines and other **gymnosperms**, the seeds are **naked**. In flowering plants, or **angiosperms**, the seeds are surrounded by the tissues of the ovary that eventually become fruits. Gymnosperms produce the male and female gametes within cones. Male gametes are called **pollen** and are light enough to ride wind currents to their final destination on a female cone. Some angiosperms like grasses are also wind pollinated, but many more have formed associations with insects to get pollen from male to female plants. The insects often get a nutritious nectar or pollen food reward in the process.

Seeds contain stored food for development of the young plant. In gymnosperms, the embryo is often surrounded by a food supply. In many angiosperms, all or part of the food supply is retained in the first leaves, called **cotyledons**. Angiosperms with no embryonic leaf, like corn and other grasses, are called **monocots**. **Dicots** like beans have two cotyledons.

BASIC FLOWER

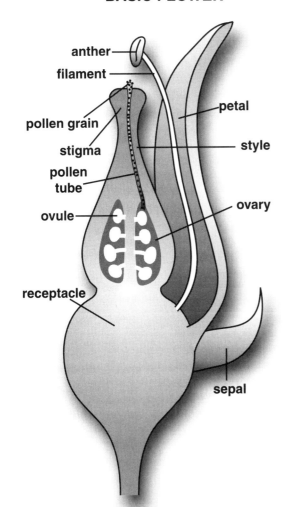

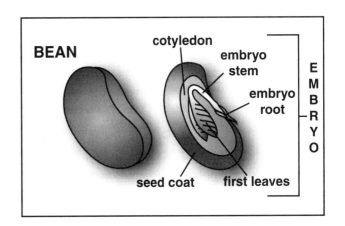

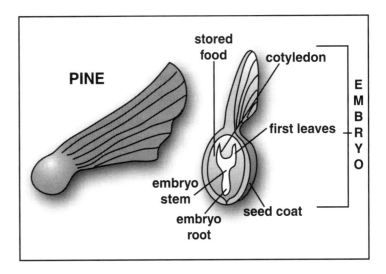

DNA: Life's Blueprint Molecule

It's easy to see family resemblances. You may have your mother's eyes, your dad's disposition, or even Uncle Oscar's nose. This passing of physical and character traits from one generation to another is called **heredity. Genetics** is the science of heredity. What chemical or combination of chemicals is responsible for this transference? One of the early guesses was that it must be some sort of protein, as proteins have a great deal of complexity and variety—something it seemed as if the units of heredity should have.

By the end of the nineteenth century, scientists were convinced that the units of heredity most likely resided in the cell's nucleus. After all, the male sperm was nothing much more than a nucleus with a tail, and males and females seemed to contribute equally to inheritance. Moreover, by this time, scientists were aware of the details of mitosis and meiosis. They knew that chromosomes halved their number during meiosis and seemed to randomly assort—in other words, each chromosome pair separated without regard to what other chromosome pairs were doing, which was consistent with observations of inheritance we will discuss shortly. Thus, the **chromosome theory** postulated that the genetic molecule was contained within chromosomes.

Sometimes more than 50% of the dry weight of a cell is made up of nucleic acids. Many of these acids reside in the nucleus—particularly **deoxyribonucleic acid**, or **DNA**. For a time, the race was on to discover this molecule's three-dimensional structure and whether that structure would provide clues as to how DNA does its job. The race was won by Francis Crick and James Watson in 1953. They provided a convincing model of DNA structure.

DNA consists of two strands of a sugar-phosphate chain, twisted about each other like a spiral staircase and linked in the middle by four nitrogen bases: **adenine**, **guanine**, **thymine**, and **cytosine**, usually just abbreviated **A**, **G**, **T**, and **C**. Adenine always pairs with thymine, and guanine always pairs with cytosine.

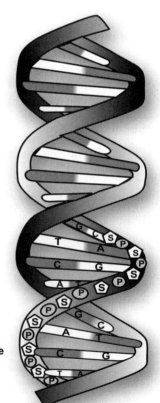

S = Sugar
P = Phosphate

A = Adenine
T = Thymine
C = Cytosine
G = Guanine

DNA: Life's Blueprint Molecule (cont.)

Watson and Crick also realized that this molecule's structure provided an easy means of self-replication—something the genetic material would have to be able to do. When the strands pull apart, each strand can act as the template for creating its complementary strand. (See below.)

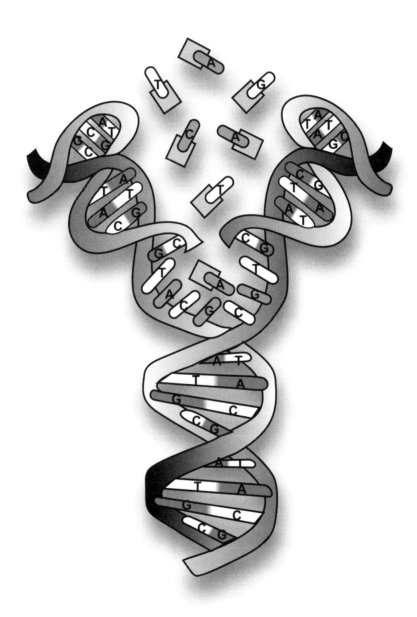

Heredity: Passing Along the Patterns

A little-known Austrian monk named **Gregor Mendel**, who possessed a flair for math, puzzled out the nature of heredity before the details of meiosis and the structure of DNA were known. He did so with pea plants and careful observations. He was fortunate to have focused on certain traits of the pea plant that were inherited in a straightforward way. Had he started with different traits, his results might not have been so impressive and clear-cut.

Mendel observed that if he crossed yellow-seeded pea plants with green-seeded pea plants, all of the succeeding generation were yellow-seeded. The traits didn't blend. Yellow-seededness seemed to dominate green-seededness. He quickly discovered, however, that the blueprint for making green seeds was not lost. If he crossed this first generation of **hybrid** plants with each other, he got yellow-seeded plants and green-seeded plants in a 3 to 1 ratio. The green-seeded trait survived, but seemed to be covered up when in the presence of the yellow-seeded trait. He said that yellow-seededness was a **dominant** trait; green-seededness was **recessive**.

How would this work? Let's call yellow-seededness *Y* and green-seededness *y*. The original plant strains he crossed were purebred strains. If each parent plant contained two hereditary units, the yellow-seeded plants would be *YY* and the green-seeded plants would be *yy*. When they crossed, each parent would contribute one hereditary unit to the offspring, so the hybrid generation would be *Yy*. Since yellowness dominates greenness in the appearance or **phenotype** of the plants, all of this generation is yellow, even though their **genotype** is *Yy*.

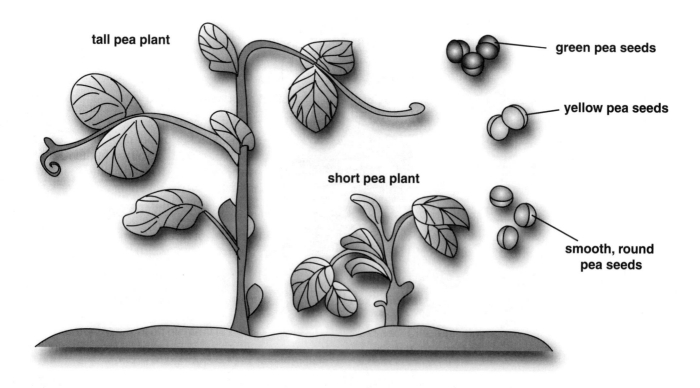

Heredity: Passing Along the Patterns (cont.)

But let's see what happens when hybrids mate. Both parents can contribute either a *Y* or a *y* to their egg or sperm. They come together in the following way:

Yellow Hybrid Parent
Genotype *Yy*

Yellow Hybrid Parent Genotype *Yy*

gametes	*Y*	*y*
Y	*YY* (yellow)	*Yy* (yellow)
y	*yY* (yellow)	*yy* (green)

Punnett Square

Approximately one-fourth will be *YY* (yellow) and one-fourth *yy* (green). The remaining one-half will be *Yy* (yellow). Thus, the ratio three-fourths yellow to one-fourth green that Mendel got in his crosses agrees with the above model.

Mendel repeated his work with thousands of pure and hybrid strains of peas, looking at seven separate traits, including seed shape, seed coat color, pod shape, pod color, flower position, and stem length. All of these studies supported the idea that hereditary traits were transmitted across the generations as discrete units that didn't "blend" or get destroyed in the process. Fifty years would pass before the details of meiosis would provide a plausible mechanism for how this occurred and many more years until DNA was pegged as the chemical that actually made up these hereditary units.

Life Throughout Time

 Thomas Jefferson, the third President of the United States, was amazed to find the skeletons of strange elephants in Kentucky. Farmers and ranchers in eastern Colorado often find the shells of sea creatures that were turned to stone on their property. These and other **fossils**—the remains of once-living creatures—found worldwide reveal several things to scientists:

1. Some entire kinds of organisms no longer exist. They have become **extinct**. In fact, about 99% of all creatures that have ever lived are now extinct.

2. Creatures that lived in the past show structural similarities to modern forms. Even though a woolly mammoth was not an African or Asian elephant, it was obviously an elephant of some kind.

3. Ancient life differs the most from modern forms in the oldest layers of rock.

Extinctions, Biodiversity, and the Future of the Human Race

 While extinctions are common on Earth, **mass extinctions** are fairly rare. Causes vary from short-term events like massive volcanic eruption and asteroid impacts to long-term processes like the slow drift of continents on the conveyor belt of Earth's hot interior, the rise and fall of oceans, and oscillations in Earth's spin and orbital characteristics. All of these events either alter climate in severe ways or change the composition of the atmosphere so that life has little time to adapt.

Which creatures survive mass extinctions? Sometimes simple chance may play a large role. The particular character of the crisis makes a difference. But in general, small adaptable animals with a varied diet would seem to have an advantage, as do plants that can go dormant for some time and come back from surviving seeds. Worldwide, the more healthy and diverse the biosphere is in terms of number and kinds of species, the more likely some hardy forms will survive.

Humans are not exempt from mass extinctions, whether caused by unpredictable events like an asteroid impact or by overuse of resources and diminished **biodiversity**. As creatures who have specialized in complex intelligence to survive, we would do well to use that intelligence to maintain a rich and healthy biosphere.

Name: _____ Date: _____

 # Part 4: Descent and Change: Putting It All Together

CONTENT REVIEW

1. T or F? An egg cell is one kind of gamete resulting from meiosis.

2. Ova are released from _____ within a woman's ovaries and pass down a _____ tube to reach the uterus.

3. During complete metamorphosis, an insect transforms from larva to adult during a sedentary phase called the _____.

4. T or F? After eight weeks of development, a young human is called an embryo.

5. "Naked seed" plants are called _____, whereas plants where the seeds are protected by plant ovarian tissue are called _____.

6. DNA is a shorthand abbreviation for _____.

7. T or F? The color phenotype of the first hybrid generation of two purebred strains of peas will be the same as its parent carrying the recessive gene for color.

8. T or F? Extinctions happen on a regular basis.

CONCEPT REVIEW

1. Explain the advantages a human embryo has to develop completely compared to a crocodile embryo. _____

   _____

2. Why is meiosis referred to as "reduction division"? _____

   _____

3. In what developmental stage of human development does menopause occur?

   _____

4. The (sporophyte/gametophyte) generation of a fern plant would be most likely to be preserved as a fossil. (Circle the answer.)

5. If you analyzed a strand of DNA and the sequence of bases was A-A-G-C-T-A, what would the sequence be on its complementary strand? ___ ___ ___ ___ ___ ___

6. If Marvin has brown eyes with a genotype of *Bb* and his wife Naomi has blue eyes of a genotype *bb*, and brown eyes is dominant to blue eyes, what percentage of their children will be blue-eyed? _____

Answer Keys

Making Sense of Life's Diversity (p. 2)
1–2.   Answers will vary.
3. Answers will vary, but could include birds, bats, insects, and humans. Birds, bats, insects, and humans vary greatly in body structure.
4. Carolus Linnaeus and Georges Cuvier

Classifying and Naming Living Things (p. 3)
1. C; A & D   2. C   3. A

Rhythms and Cycles in the Biosphere (p. 11)
1. Evaporation, condensation, precipitation
2. Producers create the oxygen needed by consumers, and consumers produce the carbon dioxide needed by producers.
3. They break down complex nitrogen compounds into forms that can be used by plants.

Ecological Succession and Biomes (p. 12)
1. The progressive change of biological communities in a given habitat resulting in a climax community
2. Deciduous forests, coniferous forests, tundra, tropical forests, grasslands, desert
3. Answers will vary.

Conservation and Biodiversity (p. 13)
1. Answers will vary.
2. Pollution: accumulation of potentially harmful substances in an environment. Sources will vary, but some possibilities are: car exhaust, factory emissions, pesticide runoff, wastes dumped in water, etc.
3. The number and kinds of organisms in an ecosystem; communities are more stable when biodiversity is high.

Part 1: Patterns in the Living World: Putting It All Together (p. 14–15)
CONTENT REVIEW:
1. structure
2. binomial nomenclature; genus, species
3. C   4. F   5. fungi   6. T   7. water
8. biological clocks   9. cold, dry   10. F
CONCEPT REVIEW:
1. T   2. B   3. nitrogen   4. T   5. F
6. Monera   7. A
8. A. species, B. genus, C. family, D. order, E. class, F. phylum, G. kingdom

Part 2: Energy Flow in Living Systems: Putting It All Together (p. 21)
CONTENT REVIEW:
1. F   2. food, water, energy, space, temperature
3. cell walls, chloroplasts   4. C   5. T
CONCEPT REVIEW:
1. T   2. Under low oxygen conditions
3. Both are made of protein   4. F   5. B

Part 3: The Human Animal and Levels of Organization: Humans' Place in Nature (p. 22)
1. F   2. Primates   3. Homo   4. A

Diseases: Infectious or Not? (p. 31)
1. (In any order) Growing so much that host functions are altered; producing poisons (toxins); destroying host tissue
2. Soap and water destroys microbes on hands, a common source of disease transmission.
3. cancer, diabetes mellitus, heart disease, vitamin deficiency diseases (any three)

Part 3: The Human Animal and Levels of Organization: Putting It All Together (p. 33–34)
CONTENT REVIEW:
1. F   2. cell, tissue, organ, organ system
3. Ligaments, tendons   4. F   5. B   6. T
7. alveoli   8.   brain, spinal cord
9. hormones   10.   non-infectious   11. F
CONCEPT REVIEW:
1. C   2. T   3. A
4. The person's other kidney can handle the functions.
5. problems with blood not clotting   6. fats
7. It would affect blood cell production.   8. organ

Part 4: Descent and Change: Putting It All Together (p. 45)
CONTENT REVIEW:
1. T   2. follicles, fallopian   3. pupa   4. F
5. gymnosperms, angiosperms
6. deoxyribonucleic acid
7. F   8. T
CONCEPT REVIEW:
1. The human embryo is protected long-term by the mother and receives food, water, and waste-removal services.
2. The number of chromosomes in sex cells are halved.
3. Adult   4. sporophyte
5. T-T-C-G-A-T   6. 50%